Great Explorers

JOHN WESLEY POWELL

Stephen Krensky

A Crabtree Crown Book

Crabtree Publishing
crabtreebooks.com

School-to-Home Support for Caregivers and Teachers

This appealing book is designed to teach students about core subject areas. Students will build upon what they already know about the subject, and engage in topics that they want to learn more about. Here are a few guiding questions to help readers build their comprehensions skills. Possible answers appear here in red.

Before Reading:

What do I know about this topic?

- *I know that John Wesley Powell explored the Colorado River and Grand Canyon.*
- *I know that Lake Powell in Utah is named after John Wesley Powell.*

What do I want to learn about this topic?

- *I want to learn how many miles John Wesley Powell and his crew traveled.*
- *I want to know what Powell and his companions thought about the beauty of the Grand Canyon.*

During Reading:

I'm curious to know...

- *I'm curious to know about the food eaten by Powell and his crew.*
- *I'm curious to know how many men survived the expedition.*

How is this like something I already know?

- *I know that riding a boat over river rapids can be very dangerous.*
- *I know that it takes courage to explore new rivers and lands.*

After Reading:

What was the author trying to teach me?

- *I think the author was trying to teach me about the challenges Powell faced on the Colorado River.*
- *I think the author was trying to teach me about the explorers who traveled West.*

How did the photographs and captions help me understand more?

- *The maps helped show me where John Wesley Powell traveled with his crew.*
- *The picture of the river showed me how rough the water was and how brave the crew must have been.*

Table of Contents

Chapter 1: A Crazy Idea

A lot of people thought John Wesley Powell was crazy. It didn't matter if they knew him well or hardly at all. They just couldn't believe he really wanted to explore the full length of the Colorado River.

John Wesley Powell

No one they knew of had ever tried this before. And who was Powell to be the first? At the age of thirty-five, he wasn't an experienced explorer. He was a former geology professor with no support from government or professional organizations. He had sold almost everything he owned to fund the trip by himself. He had even borrowed the scientific instruments he needed because he could not afford to buy them himself.

If all that wasn't enough, there was another thing standing in his way. Powell had only one good arm. As a sergeant-major during the Civil War, he had lost most of his right arm during the Battle of Shiloh in April 1862.

John Wesley Powell in the Civil War

Chapter 2: Learning the Ropes

Of course, Powell did not focus on the barriers standing in his way. For him, having one arm was a fact of life. He did not believe it should stop him from becoming an explorer.

Powell had already been exploring the natural world his whole life. Born in 1834, he had wandered as a boy in the countryside near his Ohio home. In 1855, when he was 20, he had spent four months walking across Wisconsin just to see what he could see.

Over the next two years he had rowed almost a 1,000 miles (1,609 km) down the Ohio River from Pittsburgh to the Mississippi River. He also took other river trips that were as long or longer. He collected shells and rocks and anything else that caught his eye.

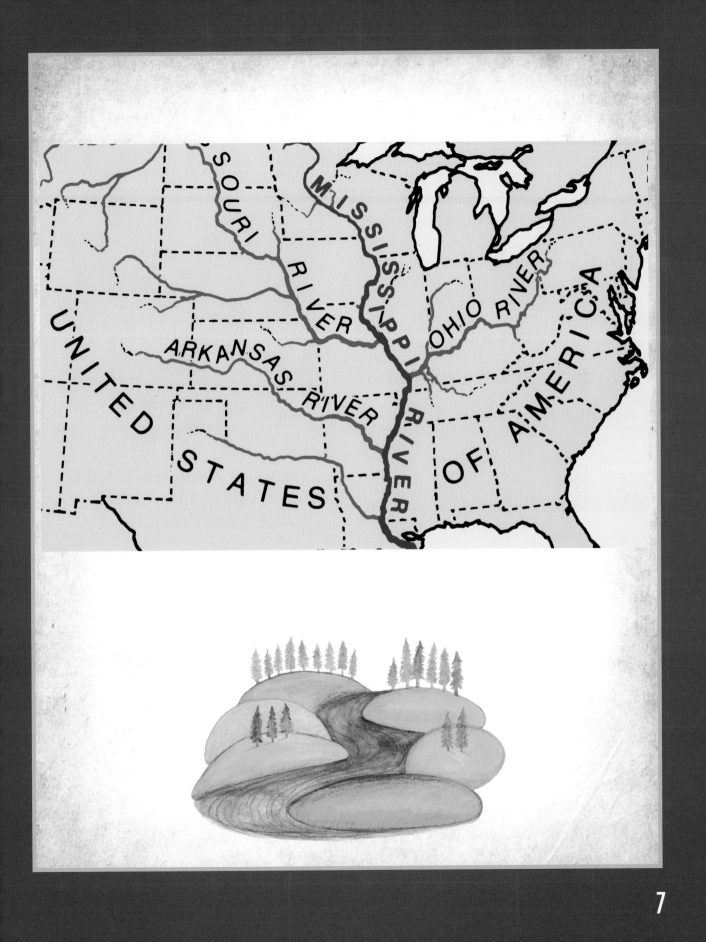

After the Civil War ended, a lot of people had advised Powell to accept his physical limitations and settle down. He took a job teaching at a local college. At the same time, he also set up and curated a small museum of scientific curiosities.

Major John Wesley Powell (right), age 31, with his brother William Bramwell Powell (left), age 29

But Powell had the itch to do more. So, in the summer of 1867, he helped lead some students on a field trip to Colorado. It was 900 miles (1,448 km) each way, and not an easy journey. Powell and his group went from railroad train to wagon train to horseback.

In Colorado, they wandered among the forests and fields and climbed Pike's Peak. Then, one night, their guide spoke of the vast canyons that lined the Colorado River, which flowed from its headwaters in the Rocky Mountains down through Colorado and Utah into Arizona and beyond. It was estimated to be well over 1,000 miles (1,609 km) long, and there were stories of people who had **ventured** down the river—and never returned. While much of the West had been investigated and mapped, that area remained largely a mystery.

Powell was captivated. It didn't matter that other people had disappeared attempting the trip. It only mattered that he was going to try it for himself.

Chapter 3: The Trip Begins

So there Powell was, two years later in May, on the banks of the river in Green River Station, Wyoming. He was leading a party of nine other men. They were going to travel in four boats that had been specially built and shipped all the way from Chicago. The boats even had names—Emma Dean, Kitty Clyde's Sister, Maid of the Canyon, and No Name.

Powell's party embarking on their journey

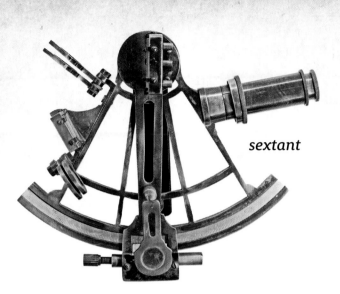

sextant

They had packed food for a ten-month journey, clothing for every kind of weather, as well as axes, hammers, and saws. Most importantly, they had "two **sextants**, four **chronometers**, a number of barometers, thermometers, compasses, and other instruments," Powell later wrote. With these, they planned to make a great many scientific observations.

"The good people of Green River City turn out to see us start," Wes wrote in his journal. "We raise our little flag, push the boats from shore, and the swift current carries us down."

The trip started out calmly enough, with crew facing upstream and glancing back over the shoulders to see where they were going next.

But the calm had little time to settle in.

Men in first camp on Green River, Wyoming, during exploration

The crew faced their first rapids a few days later, always on the lookout for a clean **chute** through which they could pass. The water often moved swiftly, and side currents **buffeted** the boats. At other times they were hit with **broadsides**—and everyone on board hung on as best they could.

On June 9th, the boats entered deeper water. They passed through a dark passage they named the Gates of Lodore. There was no way to see the danger up ahead. It was too late when Wes suddenly realized the threat and called for them to stop.

The first fall was only about 10 feet (3 m), which they could survive well enough.

But then the river tumbled again for another 50 feet (15 m).

One of the boats, the No-Name, struck one rock as it fell. Then it struck another, and finally hit a third before breaking in the middle. The men on board were thrown into the water and escaped, but their supplies were not so lucky.

It was easy enough to name the spot Disaster Falls, but the loss was a heavy blow. They were only 16 days into their journey, and they had lost a good part of their belongings.

Still, they continued on.

Head of Disaster Falls

Not all of the crew's explorations were on the river itself. Sometimes, they would pull the boats ashore to climb a nearby peak. On one such outing, Powell walked ahead along a granite outcropping of **crags** and peaks. As he later wrote, "in my eagerness to reach a point where I can see the roaring [river] full, I go too far along the wall, and can neither advance nor retreat."

The explorer was stuck, with one foot standing on a small projecting rock while his only hand clung to a small **crevice**. Four hundred feet below, the river was waiting.

Powell's men tried to lower him a line, but with only one useful arm, Wes was stuck. If he let go of the crevice to grab the rope, he would fall.

At last, the men devised another solution using two of the boat oars. They extended one to steady Powell against the rock wall, while the other was placed to give him a spot to step free.

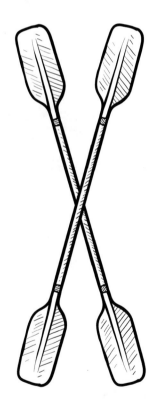

Chapter 4: Troubled Waters

On July 17th, the expedition entered the Colorado River at the junction of the Green and Grand Rivers. Other close calls followed.

John Wesley Powell's boat on the Colorado River

The river widened and narrowed. Sometimes the travelers hugged the mountain walls with their boats to avoid sharp rocks or dangerous currents. In a few places, the river looked so dangerous that the crew carried the boats out of the water and brought them downstream to a safer place to go back in.

The extreme weather tested them as well. Temperatures climbed to over 100 degrees by day and then plummeted at night, leaving the men shivering in their threadbare clothes. It was hard to determine their position. Where were they exactly? How far did they have to go?

Powell had no idea. He wrote, "we have an unknown distance yet to run, an unknown river to explore. What falls there are, we know not; what rocks beset the channel, we know not; what walls rise over the river, we know not."

When Powell and his crew finally entered what they came to call the Grand Canyon, the walls rimming the river ran up more than one mile (1.6 km) on each side. They would help take measurements that would later establish the canyon as 277 miles (446 km) long and 18 miles (29 km) wide. As amazing as the previous sights had been, the Grand Canyon clearly stood out.

"The Grand Canyon is a land of song," Wes wrote. "Mountains of music swell in the rivers, hills of music billow in the creeks, and meadows of music murmur in the rills that ripple over the rocks."

Powell entering the canyon

On August 28, the 96th day of the journey, what looked like the most dangerous rapid yet appeared before them. Three of the remaining men decided they had reached their limit. They begged Powell and the others to go ashore with them. But this invitation was politely refused.

Still, the split was friendly, and the three men left with supplies and weapons to protect themselves. Wes wrote that "some tears were shed" because each group thought the other was "taking the dangerous course."

Sadly, the three men who left the river were never heard from again.

Chapter 5: The End at Last

A few days later, Powell and his remaining men reached the end of their journey. They had faced countless hurdles and had cheated death more times than they cared to remember.

But they had succeeded at last.

Powell in 1891

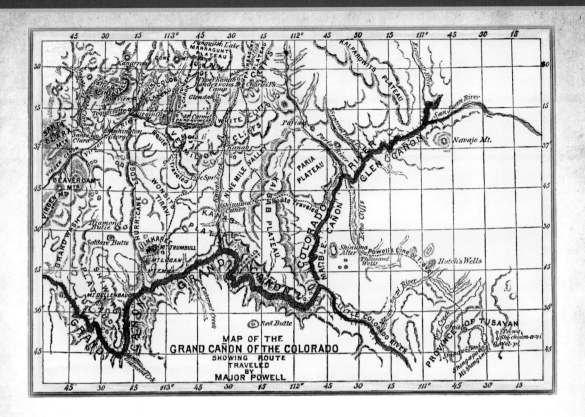

After around three months, 1,000 miles (1,609 km), and hundreds of rapids, John Wesley Powell and his remaining men had reached their goal. They were the first documented expedition to follow the Colorado River all the way to the end of the Grand Canyon.

After his safe return, Powell found himself celebrated as a national hero. He made a point of trying to describe the magnitude of what he had seen. "You cannot see the Grand Canyon in one view, as if it were a changeless spectacle from which a curtain might be lifted," he explained, "but to see it you have to toil from month to month through its **labyrinths**."

It was Powell's hope that the natural beauty of the West would be left undisturbed. But **commercial** forces continued to push successfully for its development. Still, over his long career, John Wesley Powell remained a firm believer in preserving the **fragile** beauty of the American West.

Glossary

broadside: The whole side of a ship above the water line

buffeted: Knocked from side to side

chronometers: Instruments for precisely measuring time, especially in the face of variable weather

chute: A narrow passage from one area to another

commercial: Related to commerce, or the buying and selling of goods and services

crags: Steep or rugged cliffs

crevice: A narrow opening or crack in a rock wall

fragile: Delicate and therefore easily broken or destroyed

labyrinths: Mazes, or complicated networks of paths and passages through which it is difficult to navigate

perished: Died

sextants: Scientific instruments that measure distances between objects, especially when determining altitudes

ventured: To travel with a sense of risk or daring

Index

Comprehension Questions

How did Powell injure his arm?

Where was the starting point of Powell's expedition to explore the Colorado River?

What kinds of challenges did Powell face before his journey?

About the Author

Stephen Krensky is the award-winning author of more than 150 fiction and nonfiction books for children. He and his wife Joan live in Lexington, Massachusetts, and he happily spends as much time as possible with his grown children and not-so-grown grandchildren.

Written by: Stephen Krensky
Designed by: Rhea Wallace
Series Development: James Earley
Proofreader: Janine Deschenes
Educational Consultant: Marie Lemke M.Ed.
Print Coordinator: Katherine Berti

Photo credits: Konoplotski: cover; LOC: p. 1; LOC: p. 1; LOC: p. 4; LOC: p. 5; Wiki: p. 7; LOC: p. 7; NPS: p. 8; Halit Omer: p. 9; Steve Boice: p. 10; LOC: p. 12; ANGHI: p. 13; LOC: p. 14; Cory Woodruff: p. 15; Artokoloro: p. 17; loc: p. 20; LHBLLC: p. 23; NPS: p. 23; PK289: p. 25; LOC: p. 26; North Wind Picture Archives: p. 27; Imago History Collection: p. 29;

Crabtree Publishing

crabtreebooks.com   800-387-7650

Printed in the U.S.A./012023/CG20220815

Published in Canada
Crabtree Publishing
616 Welland Ave.
St. Catharines, Ontario
L2M 5V6

Published in the United States
Crabtree Publishing
347 Fifth Ave
Suite 1402-145
New York, NY 10016

Library and Archives Canada Cataloguing in Publication
Available at Library and Archives Canada

Library of Congress Cataloging-in-Publication Data
Available at the Library of Congress

Hardcover: 978-1-0398-0015-1
Paperback: 978-1-0398-0074-8
Ebook (pdf): 978-1-0398-0193-6
Epub: 978-1-0398-0133-2